Contents

Images of Terrorism

Andy, a ninth grader, says he will always remember where he was on September 11, 2001. That was the day planes crashed into the World Trade Center towers in New York City, into the Pentagon in Washington, D.C., and in rural Pennsylvania.

"We were in homeroom," he says. "I was trying to do some last-minute studying for a history test. And then the teacher across the hall came in our room. He looked really scared. He said, 'Turn on the television;

Smoke and flames billow from the World Trade Center moments after the September 11 terrorist attack.

Understanding Issues

Terrorism

Gail B. Stewart

KIDHAVEN PRESS

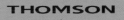

THOMSON

GALE

Detroit • New York • San Diego • San Francisco
Boston • New Haven, Conn. • Waterville, Maine
London • Munich

Library of Congress Cataloging-in-Publication Data

Stewart, Gail B., 1949–
  Terrorism / by Gail B. Stewart.
    p. cm.—(Understanding issues)
Summary: Uses the terrorist attacks of September 11, 2001, to
explore the historical, political, and religious origins of political
violence, its effects on individuals, and what governments can
do to stop it.
    ISBN 0-7377-1287-2 (hardback : alk. paper)
    1. Terrorism—Juvenile literature. [1. Terrorism. 2. Political
violence. 3. September 11 Terrorist Attacks, 2001.] I. Title.
II. Series.
    HV6431 .S746 2002
    303.6'25—dc21

2001006215

Printed in the U.S.A.

something bad has happened in New York.' When we turned the TV on, we all watched the World Trade Center [towers] burning, because two airplanes had crashed into it."

Andy says that the shots of the second plane crashing into the tower frightened him. "It was like a movie," he says. "And they kept replaying that part over and over again. A lot of the kids in my class were crying. I didn't cry, but I felt awful. I even dreamed about it that night."[1]

"I Can't Forget That Part"

Jenna was in class, too. She agrees that the footage of the planes hitting the buildings was scary. But what she remembers most was how her teachers looked that day.

"Mr. Robertson is my favorite teacher," she says. "He is fun—he makes everyone laugh. Even when he's mad, you know he still likes you. But that day he looked different; I can't really explain it. He let us watch the reports on TV and didn't say anything. He put his hands over his face and just sat there.

"I was scared then," Jenna admits. "I wanted him to tell us it would be okay. I get so scared when teachers and other grown-ups act afraid. I can't forget that part—I think I'll probably remember the look on Mr. Robertson's face that day for my whole life."[2]

"It's a Nightmare"

The attacks of September 11, 2001, were frightening for everyone—adults, teens, and younger children. At

The south side of the Pentagon burns after a hijacked jet plowed into the building.

first, no one knew who was safe and who was caught in the fire and explosion at the World Trade Center. No one knew how many people were killed in the buildings, or in the airplanes that crashed into them. No one knew at first how many died at the Pentagon, either, or in the crash in rural Pennsylvania.

In the next hours, however, the information became clear. The crashes were not accidents. The pilots did not make mistakes in flying their planes. These were attacks. People with knives took control of four airplanes. It is believed that on at least one plane, they killed the pilots and told passengers that they also had bombs. And unbelievably, the hijackers deliberately crashed the planes, knowing they would die, too.

These events were so horrible that people had a hard time understanding them. What sort of person would kill thousands of innocent people—and himself—on purpose? "It's a nightmare," sobbed one woman. "It's a nightmare, and I can't wake up."[3]

No Rules

Such terrible violence is called terrorism. Terrorism is somewhat like a war, but it is not fought between nations. Instead, terrorism involves a small group of people who wage war on a very large group, such as a government. Terrorists use violence to achieve change.

It seems as though it would not be a fair fight. Large armies usually have no trouble defeating small armies. But terrorists rarely attack a nation's army.

A woman reacts to the September 11 terrorist attacks with sadness and disbelief.

Flames engulf a car destroyed by a terrorist bomb in Tel Aviv, Israel.

Instead, they attack civilians—people who are not part of an army. Wars generally do not aim specifically at civilians, even though civilians frequently are hurt or killed.

Terrorists want their attacks to be surprises. They are secretive; they do not want to be noticed. They make their plans quietly. Such plans might mean killing the nation's president or setting fire to a school or bombing a building. They might mean **hijacking** —or taking over—an airplane, too, and taking the passengers **hostage.** Terrorists might threaten to kill everyone onboard unless their demands are met.

Terrorists want people to be afraid. The terrorists want people to put pressure on their leaders to give them what they want. If this happens, terrorists feel that they have won. By using violence and fear, they want to force governments to give in to their demands.

More than Grief

After the attacks of September 11, 2001, people in the United States were grieving. Thousands of innocent people had died. Many of them had children, who had said good-bye to their parents that morning. It started off as a regular work day. No one had any idea that so much death would happen that day.

But people felt more than sadness and grief after the attacks. They were confused, too. Everyone wanted to know who could do such a thing. Many experts soon found evidence that pointed to terrorists who live in the Middle East. These terrorists had committed other violent acts over the past few years. These acts were aimed at either the United States or its **allies**.

Within hours after the September 11 attacks, leaders of many countries called President George W. Bush. They assured him that they would help the United States find the people responsible. Tony Blair, the prime minister of Britain, said that every free nation must help stop terrorism. "We here in Britain," he promised, "stand shoulder to shoulder with our American friends in this hour of tragedy."[4]

But Who Is the Enemy?

Other leaders agreed with Tony Blair. They, too, were eager to help. However, many experts believe that fighting terrorism will be very, very hard. People who commit terrorism do not live in one country. They do not identify themselves to other people as terrorists. Fighting terrorism is almost like fighting an invisible army.

But terrorism needs to stop. People do not want to be afraid. They do not want their cities destroyed by planes. They do not want their friends and family members to be in danger.

One New York woman says she still feels very sad every day, thinking about the people who died on September 11. "I think about their children who will never see them again," she says. "I think about the brave firefighters who were killed, trying to rescue those who were hurt.

Tony Blair (left) and George W. Bush speak to reporters about plans for stopping terrorism.

The people of Seattle mourn for the victims of the
September 11 attacks.

"These were innocent people, just starting their
work day. It could have been me, you, anyone. I have
a little girl, almost two years old. I don't want her to
experience this. I don't want her to grow up in a
world where people do this to one another. Terrorism
has to end—right now."[5]

Chapter Two

Hatred and Terrorism

Terrorism is not a new problem. There have been terrorists throughout history—even in ancient Egypt, Greece, and Rome. Small groups of people who wanted to take over the government would secretly make plans. They might plot to kill the king or emperor, usually by poisoning him or stabbing him with a knife.

Often, such terrorists did not worry if they were arrested or hurt. They believed that their mission was important and their victims were evil. Even if the terrorists knew they themselves would be killed, they did not mind. One historian says, "People who use terror this way usually see everything in terms of black or white, bad or good. There are no in-betweens. Their cause is very good, and whoever gets in the way of their cause is very bad. Thinking like that is the only way they could commit such horrible crimes."[6]

Religion and Terrorism

Religion is often at the root of terrorism. That may seem strange because most religions teach love and peace. But some of the worst violence in history has been done in the name of religion. This does not mean that the religions themselves are violent. But certain terrorist leaders take ideas from a holy book and twist them around to justify violence.

Certain violent Muslim groups, for instance, believe in the idea of a **jihad,** or holy war. They say that their religion promises great rewards to those who kill nonbelievers. Special rewards are given to Muslims who die fighting in a jihad. Many people believe that the terrorists who flew planes into the

A masked gunman waves the flag of a militant Muslim group called Islamic Jihad.

World Trade Center, the Pentagon, and rural Pennsylvania were members of such groups.

Sometimes certain religions are targets of terrorists. In the 1930s Jewish people were targeted by people in Germany. Terrorists broke windows in Jewish stores and homes. They sprayed hateful slogans on Jewish temples. A large number of innocent people died, too. Many Jews fled Germany, afraid of what terrorists would do next.

Shattered glass marks Nazi violence against a Jewish-owned business in 1938.

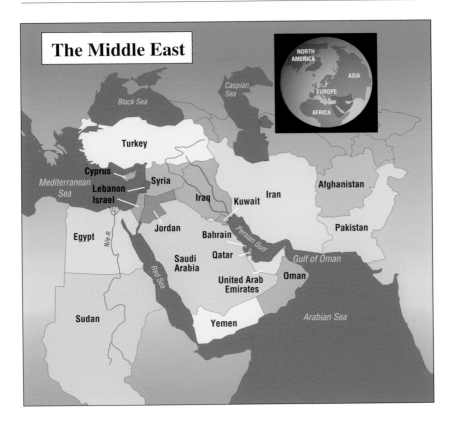

The Middle East

Terror in the Middle East

The Middle East includes countries such as Egypt, Israel, Saudi Arabia, and Iraq. It has been the scene of much of the world's terrorism in the past few decades. Some of that region's violence has been based on religion, and some on disputes over land.

The Arabs and the Jews have long been fighting over land that both groups consider holy. Extremists on both sides have used violence to try to get what they want.

Terrorists have planted car bombs on busy streets and set off bombs in busy shopping areas. Many innocent people—including children—have been killed.

Terrorism and Independence

Another motive for terrorists is independence. Many countries have groups who do not want to be ruled by the government. These groups may feel that they have no rights and that the government does not listen to them.

In 1995 a group of people in a province near Russia felt this way. Their province was controlled by the Russian army, but these people did not want to be under Russia's control. Some formed terrorist groups and armed themselves with machine guns and grenades. One group sneaked into a Russian city and set houses on fire. They blew up buses. They captured two thousand people, and held them as hostages. They said they would release them only after Russia took its army away. The fighting continued for a long time, and tens of thousands died.

Northern Ireland has also suffered a great deal of terrorism. Many people in Northern Ireland want their independence from Great Britain. However, many others prefer being ruled by Britain. Most Irish people would like to work out these problems peacefully. However, there are some people on both sides who are not patient. They do not want to have long discussions. Instead, they use terrorist acts like bombing and shooting to frighten one another.

Terrorism in the United States

The United States has been a target of terrorists, too. The frightening attacks of September 11, 2001, were the worst. But they were not the first attacks on this country. The United States has been a target for terrorists for many years, for various reasons.

The United States has been a supporter of the Jewish nation of Israel. That angers some Muslim groups. In 1983 a Muslim group of terrorists launched a truck bombing in Lebanon. The bomb blew up the U.S. Marine barracks, killing 241 marines.

The African nation of Libya has dangerous terrorists, too. One Libyan group blew up an American passenger plane in 1988. The plane was flying from London to New York when a bomb exploded. All 259 passengers were killed. Later, it was learned that Libyan groups were angry that American warplanes had attacked Libya after an earlier act of terrorism. They destroyed the plane and killed its passengers to punish the United States for that attack.

The cockpit from the airplane destroyed by a Libyan terrorist bomb in 1988 lies on the ground in Scotland.

Not Always Foreigners

Terrorism in the United States is not always the work of foreign groups. American hate groups like the Ku Klux Klan have been targeting minorities since the nineteenth century. They believe that white people are superior to other races. To frighten other groups away from white neighborhoods, Klan members have set fires to homes, schools, and businesses owned by black people. The Klan has shot or hanged many blacks, too.

Ku Klux Klan members salute a burning cross. The Klan is known for its hate crimes.

In the later years of the twentieth century, some of the Klan members joined new groups. Some of these groups were even more hateful and dangerous. They have names like the Order and Aryan Nation. They not only target blacks, but they also hate Jews, Asians, and other minorities. These hate groups hope to create a "whites only" homeland in northwestern states such as Wyoming, Montana, Washington, Idaho, and Oregon.

Besides being **racist**, these groups are antigovernment. They believe that the government interferes with their lives. Leaders of the Order and Aryan Nation collect huge stocks of guns and ammunition. They urge their members to kill anyone connected with the government. Members who kill a police officer become heroes and are given the title of "warrior."

The Oklahoma Bombing

Most of these terrorists were arrested or killed in shootouts with the FBI or police. Some people thought that their hatred would disappear, too. But they were wrong. Antigovernment hate was the reason behind one of America's most shocking crimes.

At about 9:00 A.M. on April 19, 1995, a truck carrying a homemade bomb exploded outside the government center in Oklahoma City, Oklahoma. The explosion was so powerful that it knocked much of the large building down. Many people who worked in the building were buried under tons of rubble. So were children who attended daycare in the building.

The nation was stunned. The images on television were heartbreaking: bloody children, screaming parents, and frantic rescuers. In all, 168 people died in that bombing. Nineteen of them were small children. Everyone wanted to know who could have done such a thing. Many at first assumed it was a Middle Eastern terrorist. After all, various Arab groups had been threatening American troops. And in 1993, terrorists from the Middle East had bombed the World Trade Center in New York, killing six people.

An Important Reminder

But the Oklahoma City bombing was not the work of foreign terrorists. Investigators found out it was

The ruins of the federal building in Oklahoma City after it was struck by a terrorist bomb.

Timothy McVeigh (bottom) and Terry Nichols (right) were convicted in the terrorist attack in Oklahoma City.

planned by two American men. Similar to the Order and Aryan Nation members, these two men hated the government.

The men were arrested for their crimes. It was an important reminder for the American people, said experts, that terrorism is not limited to groups from the Middle East, Northern Ireland, or other faraway places. Terrible, random killing can be caused by American people, too. And the violence their actions cause is just as horrible as that of any foreign terrorist.

Chapter Three

The Effects of Terrorism

Acts of terrorism do not affect only the people who are hurt or killed. The effects of terrorism are felt by hundreds, thousands—and sometimes millions of other people. Some of these effects happen right away. Others take a longer time to appear.

"It's Too Much Death"

In many acts of terrorism, people are hurt or killed. After the terrorist acts of September 11, 2001, thousands were missing. Experts knew that many were probably dead, but they did not want to give up hope. Rescue workers worked day and night searching for people who might still be alive under the ruins.

Sometimes there were happy endings. A firefighter was found alive, buried under piles of debris. A teenage girl who had lost track of her younger brother was excited when a rescuer found him. The boy had a broken leg and was trapped under a large piece of metal. A firefighter heard him crying, and after moving the metal, carried him to a safe place. These stories kept rescue workers hopeful that more survivors would be found. Frightened family members waited nearby, hoping for news of a loved one.

Rescuers search for survivors in the rubble of the World Trade Center.

However, as the days went by, it seemed that there would be no more survivors. By December 2001, investigators estimated that more than three thousand people had died at the World Trade Center, at the Pentagon, and in the four airplanes that crashed. So much death affected more than the families of the victims.

Entire companies were wiped out because hundreds of their employees were dead. Many rescue workers—brave firefighters, ambulance drivers, and

Firefighters salute the flag-draped coffin of a colleague who died during rescue efforts.

police who were trying to rescue victims—were killed when the towers collapsed. One New York City official said that he had been to more than fifty funerals in four days. Another man was heartsick because he had lost two sons and a nephew—all firefighters. "It's too much death,"[7] he said, his voice choked with tears.

Destruction

In addition to death, there is often destruction. Workers must clean up the rubble of buildings that have been bombed or set on fire. That can be very dangerous work. After the World Trade Center towers were destroyed, workers and others in the area wore masks. The thick clouds of smoke that billowed from the ruins were unhealthy to breathe.

The debris from an act of terrorism is often very important. After the 1988 bombing of the American plane, investigators saved every piece of the wreckage. They inspected it very carefully, looking for clues showing who was to blame. Finally, a tiny scrap of the bomb's circuit board was found. That gave investigators an idea of how and where the bomb was made. That information finally led to the identity of the terrorist group.

Fear

But terrible destruction and death are not the only effects of terrorism. Some effects are not as obvious right away, but they are just as destructive. Fear is the

Experts must reconstruct a plane in an effort to determine the cause of a crash.

effect terrorists aim for—more than killing or destroying buildings or planes. By making a nation feel frightened, terrorists have control.

Fear is a very powerful emotion. People who watched the World Trade Center towers hit by planes were afraid. They were worried that more planes were coming. Where would they crash next? Even people who did not live near New York wondered if the same thing could happen in their city.

Christy, age fourteen, lives in Minnesota, far from where the attacks of September 2001 took place. Even so, she says she has been afraid ever since that day. "I hear a plane going over, and that's the first thing I think of," she says. "It's silly in a way. Planes have always gone over my house, because we live near the airport. And they never scared me before. But now I think they're going to crash into my house, or a building nearby."[8]

Counselors say that Christy's fears are not silly or childish. Plenty of adults are frightened, too. They worry about themselves and their children. They worry that they will not be able to keep their families safe. Unfortunately, fear of terrorists can often change the way people live their lives.

Changing Lives

Any time a plane is hijacked, people worry about flying. This was especially true when hijackers crashed the planes into the World Trade Center, the Pentagon, and rural Pennsylvania. Many people canceled plans

Fear is one response to terrorism. Many Americans, including this woman and her daughter, found comfort through prayer services.

they had already made for vacations. They decided to stay home rather than to take the risk of flying.

Ken and his family were planning to visit Washington, D.C., in October 2001. However, after the attacks the month before, his parents thought about changing their plans. The idea of flying on a plane made them nervous. But at the last minute, they decided to go after all.

"I'm glad we're going," says Ken. "We've studied a lot of things about government in my class—I'm in eighth grade. I wanted to see the Lincoln Memorial and the Capitol. My dad said, 'What kind of people would we be if we were afraid to visit the capital of our country?' I know we will be nervous at first, getting on the plane. But it'll be okay."[9]

"I'm Not a Terrorist!"

Fear can have more negative effects on people than simply changing vacation plans. It can make people begin to fear one another, too. After investigators learned that Islamic terrorists were to blame for the September 2001 attacks, some Americans became nervous. They looked at people from the Middle East with suspicion, wondering if they were terrorists, too.

Some Middle Eastern people living in the United States have been called names. Some have even been attacked. Seventeen-year-old Saade was yelled at by someone in a passing car. His parents are from Syria, and though Saade dresses like most American teens, he looks Middle Eastern.

A Massachusetts man, of Iranian ancestry, cleans up the mess left by vandals.

"I was mad at first when that guy yelled at me," he says. "I mean, does he think I am a terrorist? I understand how angry everyone is now. I am angry, too. My uncle is a New Yorker, and he knows people who died that day. I just don't want all Arabs to have a bad name. I'm not a terrorist!"[10]

Looking Beyond the Fear

Counselors say that fear and anger take a toll on people's spirits. Such emotions do not help a person feel strong. Instead, they rob people of energy. Experts say that terrorism can do that—it can rob a nation of its energy and spirit. Citizens become used to feeling afraid and are not hopeful about the future.

But being afraid will not stop terrorism. The government is trying to find ways to get rid of terrorism. People in the government want to make it harder for terrorists to commit these crimes. They can come up with ways to keep airplanes and buildings safer for people. People should not ever have to worry about such horrible things happening ever again.

Shock shows on the face of a woman viewing the rubble of the World Trade Center after the terrorist attack.

A young woman lights a candle at a New York City memorial.

One writer said after the September 2001 terrorism that it is hard to imagine anything good coming from such a terrible disaster. "But the best memorial to those who perished," he wrote, "would be the achievement of a safer, saner world."[11] That sounds like a very hard job. But some people are already talking about the best ways to start.

Chapter Four

A Difficult Enemy

Terrorism is a difficult enemy to fight because many different terrorist organizations are scattered throughout the world. They rarely live within the boundaries of one nation. Instead, they operate in **cells**, or small groups of eight or ten. These cells are very secretive. They blend into the community where they live. They usually look and act just like other people. How can such terrorists be found?

Gathering Information

Some of the fight against terrorism must take place outside a country's borders. Agents travel around the world, quietly learning as much as they can about terrorists. Some of the best ammunition in this fight is information. What are the names of the groups, and how many terrorists are in each one? What sorts of weapons do they have? Where do they get the money to support their terrorism? And are there any nations who help them?

Every bit of information about a suspected terrorist is carefully entered into computers. No detail is too

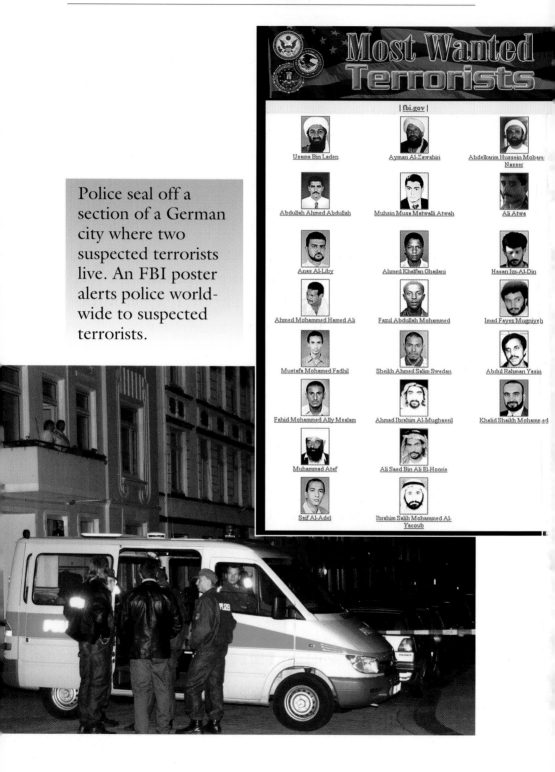

Police seal off a section of a German city where two suspected terrorists live. An FBI poster alerts police world-wide to suspected terrorists.

small. Is the person left handed? What languages does the person speak? What **aliases**, or other names, has the person used? Knowing the answers to questions like these can help agents locate suspected terrorists. New terrorist attacks can be prevented this way.

Many nations are willing to share their information. France's agents might have information that will help agents in Germany or England. German agents might have information that will help the United States or Spain. Experts say that cooperating and sharing information is very important. Terrorists need to understand that the world's governments will not tolerate such violence.

Protecting Leaders

One important part of the war against terrorism is keeping the president and other leaders safe. Over the years, terrorists have **assassinated** leaders in various countries, including some U.S. presidents. That is why important officials have bodyguards. In the United States, the president has a team of **Secret Service** agents whose job is to keep the president from harm.

Most world leaders ride in vehicles with special bulletproof glass windows, too. Even religious leaders must take special care. Ever since Pope John Paul II was shot by a Turkish terrorist in 1981, he uses a special car. It has high windows made of bulletproof glass, and it is nicknamed "The Popemobile." Even though Pope John Paul and other world leaders

Bodyguards hold Pope John Paul II after he was shot by a terrorist's bullet.

often wish they could be closer to the people, they understand that security is important.

But other targets of terrorism are important to keep safe, too. After the bombing of the government center in Oklahoma City, many federal and state buildings changed. Many put up cement barriers outside, making it impossible for a car or truck with a bomb to get close to the building. Parking spaces were moved farther from the buildings, too.

A New Kind of Airport?

Airplanes are another target of terrorists. For decades, airports around the world have checked luggage, backpacks, and purses. This is to make sure people are not bringing weapons on board that would allow them to hijack an airplane. However, hijackers—or

Travelers undergo tightened airport security checks after September 11.

people who were helping them—brought knives on the airplanes on September 11, 2001. It is clear that U.S. airport security was not strict enough.

Soon after the attacks, many changes were made. Airport security now checks passengers more carefully. Anything that could be used as a weapon is seized—even things such as scissors, shaving razors, and nail clippers. Armed guards are patrolling airports, too.

Experts say that even more security measures might be added. Dogs trained to sniff out bombs will be used. Fingerprint scanners will be used, too. Every airport worker must be scanned before he or she can get close to the airplanes. Since each person's fingerprints are unique, no terrorist will be able to get on board by pretending to be an airport worker. That way, terrorists will not be able to get close to planes. Armed air marshals now ride on many flights. They dress in regular clothes so that terrorists cannot tell if a marshal is on board.

"We're All Used to Being Free"

There are many new types of technology that can help fight terrorism, too. One is a camera system that scans a large crowd, such as those in the stands at a football game or a busy downtown street. Inside a database, or large collection of information, are pictures of people from around the world known to be terrorists. The camera system analyzes each face and quickly compares it to all the faces in the database. If a face matches, the system quickly alerts the user.

U.S. National Guardsmen provide security at a
New York airport.

New technology such as these cameras are helping
with the fight against terrorism. However, some people find these changes disturbing. They worry about
cameras scanning people, and armed soldiers in airports. They worry when the FBI listens in on telephone conversations of people who seem suspicious.
They say that those advances might violate personal
freedom.

"I visited Israel two years ago," says one woman.
"They have soldiers everywhere, guarding and watch-
ing everything. The people there don't seem to
notice it; maybe they're used to it. But the people I

was with—we were all nervous. I just can't imagine living that way here, in America."[12]

Another woman agrees. "We're all used to being free. We can get on a plane, or go somewhere for a visit, and we don't even think about it. But after the terrible attacks [on September 11, 2001] no one feels that way. You know you'll have to get to the airport real early [and] stand in line. Someone will search you and take your purse apart, looking for weapons. I

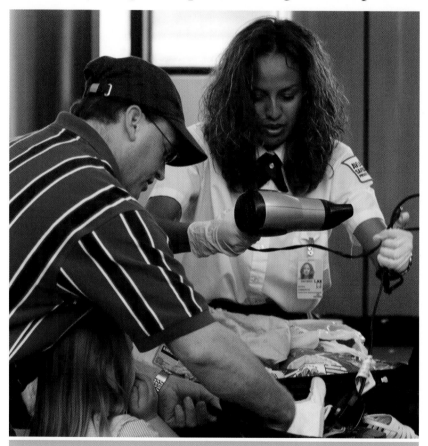

A traveler shows the contents of his luggage to an airport security worker.

don't know if I could ever get used to something like that!"[13]

"Maybe That's Not So Bad!"

But other people say they do not mind the inconveniences. They will stand in line to get searched. They will gladly have marshals on their flights. They do not object if agents want to listen in on a phone call of someone who might be a terrorist. Being safe is most important, say those people.

"I don't care about frisking and baggage checks. . . . You go to some places and see guys in [army] jackets holding machine guns, and you think, 'Whoa, this is scary,'" says one man. "Now you think, 'Whoa, maybe that's not so bad!'"[14]

Until the attack of September 2001, the United States had been fairly lucky. Very few acts of terrorism had happened on American soil. Now, however, the United States has to face the same problems as people in Northern Ireland, in Israel, in Egypt, in Russia, and in other nations. The world's fight against terrorism will be a long and difficult one. There will be important questions to answer along the way.

But it is a war that must be won.

Notes

Chapter 1: Images of Terrorism
1. Personal interview; Andy, Richfield, Minnesota, September 21, 2001.
2. Telephone interview, Jenna, September 20, 2001.
3. Quoted on CNN World Coverage, September 11, 2001.
4. Quoted in "Global Mourning," *People Weekly*, September 24, 2001, p. 68.
5. Telephone interview, Magdalene, September, 20, 2001.

Chapter 2: Hatred and Terrorism
6. Telephone interview, Kathleen Kennedy, September 23, 2001.

Chapter 3: The Effects of Terrorism
7. Quoted on CNN World Coverage, September 13, 2001.
8. Personal interview; Christy, Minneapolis, Minnesota, September 20, 2001.
9. Telephone interview, Ken, September 29, 2001.
10. Personal interview; Saade, Minneapolis, Minnesota, September 16, 2001.
11. Kenneth Auchincloss, "We Shall Overcome," *Newsweek*, September 24, 2001, p. 18.

Chapter 4: A Difficult Enemy
12. Telephone interview, Jeanne, September 21, 2001.
13. Personal interview, Grace, St. Paul, Minnesota, September 30, 2001.
14. Quoted in "Will We Ever Be Safe Again?" *Newsweek*, September 24, 2001, p. 61.

Glossary

alias: A phony name.

allies: Nations that are friendly to another nation.

assassinate: To plan and murder an important leader.

cell: A small group of terrorists working closely together.

hijacking: To take over an airplane during its flight and use it for terrorist purposes.

hostage: A person seized during a hijacking or other crime, to be used as a bargaining tool.

jihad: A war that is considered to be holy by Muslim extremists.

racist: A person who makes negative judgments about another person based on his or her race or ethnic background.

Secret Service: A group of people who guard and protect the U.S. president, vice president, and their families.

For Further Exploration

Ann G. Gaines, *Terrorism*. Philadelphia: Chelsea House, 1999. Very well written with an excellent index.

Keith Greenberg, *Terrorism: The New Menace*. Brookfield, CT: Millbrook, 1994. Good information on fighting terrorism; quality photographs.

Alison Jamieson, *Terrorism*. New York: Thompson Learning, 1995. Includes a section about terrorism in Northern Ireland.

Victoria Sherrow, *The World Trade Center Bombing*. Springfield, NJ: Enslow, 1998. Easy reading, with good information on the 1993 bombing.

Philip Steele, *Terrorism*. New York: New Discovery, 1992. Challenging reading, but a helpful glossary.

Index

Picture Credits

About the Author

Gail B. Stewart has written over ninety books for young people, including a series for Lucent Books called The Other America. She has written many books on historical topics such as World War I and the Warsaw ghetto.

Stewart received her undergraduate degree from Gustavus Adolphus College in St. Peter, Minnesota. She did her graduate work in English, linguistics, and curriculum study at the College of St. Thomas and the University of Minnesota. She taught English and reading for more than ten years. Stewart and her husband live in Minneapolis with their three sons.